INSIDE THE
SUPER BOWL

BY TODD KORTEMEIER

Published by The Child's World®
1980 Lookout Drive • Mankato, MN 56003-1705
800-599-READ • www.childsworld.com

Acknowledgments
The Child's World®: Mary Berendes, Publishing Director
Red Line Editorial: Design, editorial direction, and production
Photographs ©: Ben Liebenberg/AP Images, cover, 1; Ric Tapia/Icon Sportswire, 5;
Pat Wellenbach/AP Images, 6; Bettmann/Corbis, 9; Rhona Wise/Icon Sportswire,
10; Charlie Riedel/AP Images, 13; Ross D. Franklin/AP Images, 14; David J. Phillip/
AP Images, 16; Kevin Terrell/AP Images, 18; Rich Graessle/Icon Sportswire, 20; Orlin
Wagner/AP Images, 23; Orlando Ramirez/Icon Sportswire, 24; Kathy Willens/AP
Images, 27; Matt Rourke/AP Images, 28

ISBN 9781634074384

LCCN 2015946276

Printed in the United States of America
Mankato, MN
December, 2015
PA02283

ABOUT THE AUTHOR

Todd Kortemeier is a writer and journalist from Minneapolis.
He is a graduate of the University of Minnesota's School of
Journalism & Mass Communication.

TABLE OF
CONTENTS

FAST FACTS

What is it? The Super Bowl matches the winners of the American Football **Conference** (AFC) and National Football Conference (NFC) to determine the champion of the National Football League (NFL).

What do they play for? The winner gets the Vince Lombardi Trophy. Lombardi was a coach. He won the first two Super Bowls, after the 1966 and 1967 seasons, with the Green Bay Packers. The trophy is made of sterling silver. It is 20.75 inches (52.7 cm) tall. Winning players also get a ring.

When is it? The Super Bowl has been played on the first Sunday in February since 2004. Before that, it was usually played in January.

Where is it? Cities bid to host the Super Bowl. A quality stadium is a big factor for selection. Cities must also be able to host other parties and events leading up to the Super Bowl. Warm cities usually get top priority. But cold cities with domed stadiums are sometimes chosen.

When was the first one? The first Super Bowl, played after the 1966 season, took place on January 15, 1967. It was held at Memorial Coliseum in Los Angeles. The Packers beat the Kansas City Chiefs 35–10.

How many people go? Super Bowl attendance is limited only by stadium capacity. The Super Bowl after the 1979 season holds the record for most spectators. The Pittsburgh

Steelers beat the Los Angeles Rams 31–19 in front of 103,985 people.

How many people watch? More than 114 million people in the United States watched the Super Bowl on February 1, 2015. That set a record for the most-watched television program in U.S. history. Advertising in front of so many viewers is expensive. Companies paid up to $4.5 million for a 30-second commercial in 2015.

Chapter 1

THE FANS' PERSPECTIVE: THE SUPER BOWL STREAK

Don Crisman and Stan Whitaker thought they were the only ones. The two friends had been to every single Super Bowl together. In 1987, they headed to their 21st edition of the big game. It was being held at the Rose Bowl in Pasadena, California. The game was their main event. But they took a side trip near Los Angeles. They went to see *The Tonight Show Starring Johnny Carson*.

There they met Tom Henschel. It turned out he had never missed a Super Bowl, either. That was when The Never Miss a Super Bowl Club was born. The three fans continued going to Super Bowls. They did not always sit together. But they were always there.

The three men then met Larry Jacobson in the late 1990s. A few years after that, Robert Cook joined the group. The five friends were at every Super Bowl from then until 2009. That year

◄ **Don Crisman is one of the founding members of The Never Miss a Super Bowl Club.**

Whitaker dropped out for health reasons. Cook passed away in 2011. Despite losing them, the three remaining members kept going. Jacobson hoped to keep the **streak** intact for as long as possible.

"Yeah, I have a goal: To go to the Super Bowl until they throw dirt on me," Jacobson said in 2011. Asking how long he wants to go is "like asking how many years you want to live or how many years you want to be married."[1]

The men did not set out to go to every Super Bowl. It just happened that way.

Henschel said he was simply in the right place at the right time. In 1967, he went to the first Super Bowl. "After I'd been to four or five, I decided I'm not going to miss this," he said.[2]

"The tickets were easy to come by," Crisman said. "I think the other part was I had this feeling that this could turn into the World Series of football. And I think I was correct."[3]

Tickets for the first Super Bowl cost just $12 in 1967. Henschel's tickets in 2015 cost $1,500 each.

Jacobson brought a date to his first Super Bowl. "She wasn't impressed with either the Super Bowl or with me," he said, "but I was impressed with the Super Bowl."[4] He brought a different date to the Super Bowl after the 1976 season. He eventually married her.

▲ The Green Bay Packers beat the Kansas City Chiefs 35-10 in the first Super Bowl.

"I just enjoy the games so much and I enjoy all the hype and excitement and seeing the celebrities that go to the games," Henschel said.[5] He said the game is like New Year's and the Fourth of July mixed together.

The club members have their own favorite teams. But above all, they are fans of football. And the Super Bowl is football's biggest event.

Chapter 2

A PLAYER'S PERSPECTIVE: THE GIANTS' DAVID TYREE

Before the Super Bowl on February 3, 2008, the play had a name. In the New York Giants' playbook, it was called 62 Y Sail Union. It would be part of one of the greatest plays in Super Bowl history.

New York Giants wide receiver David Tyree was not a superstar. He was a valuable special teams player. He made the **Pro Bowl** in that role in 2005. But he had made more tackles than catches during the 2007 season before the Super Bowl.

As the season went along, Tyree started contributing more on offense. "All of [a] sudden, last two games of the year," he said, "I'm in the mix."[6]

The Super Bowl is always a big challenge. For the Giants, this one was even bigger than usual. Their opponents were the New England Patriots. The Patriots were 18–0 entering the game.

◀ **New York Giants wide receiver David Tyree (85) became a Super Bowl hero in 2008.**

Only one other NFL team had ever won the Super Bowl to finish the season undefeated.

The Super Bowl is often played two weeks after the conference championship games. In 2008, those two weeks were filled mostly with talk about the Patriots.

"Everywhere you went, it was all about the Patriots and 19–0," Giants cornerback R. W. McQuarters said.[7]

But the Giants had something to say about that. New York's defensive front kept the Patriots' record-setting offense in check. New England led 7–3 after three quarters.

New York's comeback started early in the fourth. Tyree made his first big play. He caught a touchdown pass from quarterback Eli Manning with 11:05 left in the game. His first touchdown catch of the year came at a great time.

But Patriots wide receiver Randy Moss caught a touchdown with 2:42 to go. The extra point put New England ahead 14–10. The Giants had one good chance for another comeback **drive**. They got to their own 44-yard line with just over a minute to go in the game. It was third down and five. The play call came in from the sideline: 62 Y Sail Union.

"[It was] just a dummy route," Tyree said.[8] That meant the ball was not supposed to be thrown to him.

▲ Tyree caught his fifth and final career touchdown in the fourth quarter of the 2008 Super Bowl.

But the play broke down. Manning was in trouble. The Patriots defense was close to **sacking** him.

"He was obviously struggling," Tyree said. "I felt open. But I knew I wasn't going to be open long."[9]

Tyree ran to the middle of the field. He got inside position on his defender. Manning saw him and threw the ball. Tyree jumped and stretched his arms upward. He grabbed the ball with two hands. Patriots **safety** Rodney Harrison tried to knock away the ball. But Tyree pinned the ball against his helmet with one hand to keep it secure. It was a 32-yard miracle catch. The Giants were still alive.

Four plays later, Manning threw a 13-yard touchdown pass to wide receiver Plaxico Burress. The Giants were Super Bowl champions. It would not have happened without Tyree.

It was his last NFL catch. Tyree retired in 2009, knowing he had accomplished a lot in his short career.

"I had won a Super Bowl," Tyree later said. "I had what some called the greatest play in Super Bowl history. What more could I really ask for?"[10]

Plaxico Burress's game-winning touchdown catch that ▶ clinched the Super Bowl was set up by Tyree's great play.

Chapter 3

THE PERFORMERS' PERSPECTIVE: U2

The first title game between the American Football League (AFL) and NFL champions was set to take place in 1967. The game was not yet known as the Super Bowl. In the months leading up to the game, a suggestion for an extravagant halftime show was made to NFL Commissioner Pete Rozelle.

"Why would we spend all that money?" Rozelle said. "That's when everybody goes to the bathroom."[11]

Flash forward to 2015. Singer Katy Perry's halftime performance drew 118.5 million viewers. That was more than four million more viewers than the game had. The Super Bowl halftime show has become a major spectacle.

Back in 2002, a huge halftime show was planned. Pop star Janet Jackson was scheduled to perform. But terrorists used airplanes to attack the United States on September 11, 2001.

◀ **U2 lead singer Bono performs during the Super Bowl on February 3, 2002.**

De_orah Welsh   William Cashman   Wilson "Bud" Flagg
Christian Adams   Georgine R. Corrigan   Darlene Flagg

World Trade Center

Richard Gabriel
Ian Gray

Gordon McCannel Aamoth   Jack Charles Aron   Stanley Hall
Maria Rose Abad   Joshua Aron   Bryan Jack
Edelmiro Abad   Richard Avery Aronow   Steven D. Jacoby
Vincent Abate   Japhet J. Aryee   Ann Judge
Andrew A. Abate   Carl Asaro   Chandler Keller
Laurence Abel   Michael A. Asciak   Yvonne Kennedy
William Abrahamson   Michael E. Asher   Norma Khan
Richard A. Aceto   Janice Ashley   Karen A. Kincaid
Erica Van Acker   Thomas J. Ashton   Dong Lee
Heinrich B. Ackermann   Manuel O. Asitimbay   Dora Menchaca
Paul A. Acquaviva   Lt. Gregg A. Atlas   Christopher Newton
Patrick Adams   Debbie Atlas-Bellows   Barbara Olson
Shannon Lewis Adams   Gerald Atwood   Ruben Ornedo
Stephen Adams   James Audiffred   Robert Penniger
Donald L. Adams   Kenneth W. Van Auken   Robert R. Ploger
Ignatius Adanga   Frank Louis Aversano   Lisa Raines

▲ **Names of victims of the September 11, 2001, terrorist attack scroll during U2's halftime performance.**

Jackson feared for her safety. She refused to travel. Many others felt the same.

NFL marketing executive John Collins was put in charge of finding a replacement. The same day he was given the task, he saw Irish rock band U2 perform in New York City. Collins was struck by a particular moment late in their show. They projected a list of the names of the September 11 victims on the roof of the arena. It was an emotional tribute. He realized U2 was perfect for the halftime show.

He pitched the idea the next day. The league and the band were excited about it. U2 would do the same tribute at the Super Bowl. But organizers ran into trouble. They could not find enough electrical power to project the names. The organizers managed to find a generator that would do the job. But some people in the league still thought the show would be terrible.

The show instead went off without a hitch. The names were projected onto giant screens behind the band. At the end, lead singer Bono opened his jacket to reveal an American flag lining. It was not just a great halftime show. It was a major cultural event.

"The greatest halftime show in the history of sporting events, hands down," reported the *Boston Globe*.[12]

Collins got a note in the mail the next day. It was from U2's manager.

"I feel sorry for whoever's next," the note said.[13]

Chapter 4

A REFEREE'S PERSPECTIVE: BILL VINOVICH

Bill Vinovich thought he might never again step foot on a NFL field. It was 2007, and Vinovich had just finished his third year as a NFL referee when a medical condition sidelined him.

"They said they weren't going to allow me on the field anymore," Vinovich said, "ever."[14]

But he did not give up. He worked in some off-field roles, such as **replay** official. Then in 2011, he had surgery to try to get healthy enough to referee again. He reapplied to the NFL in 2012 and was approved. Vinovich was great during his first season back. He was selected to referee in the playoffs. Then he was named a Super Bowl alternate.

Referees are chosen for the Super Bowl based on performance. Vinovich was again chosen for the playoffs in 2015. There, it was a call he actually did not make that showed he was ready for

◄ **Referee Bill Vinovich makes a call during the Super Bowl on February 1, 2015.**

Super Bowl selection. It was during a playoff matchup between the Baltimore Ravens and the New England Patriots. On a key play, the Patriots used a brand new **formation**. It looked strange. But in just seconds, Vinovich realized the unique formation was still legal. He allowed play to continue. Vinovich's boss, Dean Blandino, said Vinovich handled it perfectly.

"He was calm, he was smooth, he was in control," Blandino said. "That's what you want an official to be in that circumstance."[15]

Vinovich heard from Blandino shortly after that game.

"I've got a couple of games left," Blandino said, "and I want to know if you want to officiate the last one."

"Are you kidding?" Vinovich said.

"I'm serious," Blandino said. "You had a great season and you controlled all your games. We're happy to have you do the game."[16]

Vinovich cried. Officiating the Super Bowl was the highest honor for a referee. But it came with a lot of pressure. Going into the game, the Patriots were under extra scrutiny. They had been accused of improperly deflating footballs in the AFC Championship Game. It was just another thing Vinovich had to keep an eye on.

▲ **Vinovich (white hat) performs the coin flip before an October 28, 2012, game during his first season back as a referee.**

"The NFL is being scrutinized," Blandino said, "and we're at the pinnacle of our game, the Super Bowl, and everything will be magnified."[17]

Before the game, Vinovich was asked if it had hit him that he was about to referee the Super Bowl.

"No, and I don't think it will until I do the coin toss, honestly," he said. "I just want to get that over with, because then it's just football."[18]

Chapter 5

A COACH'S PERSPECTIVE: THE SEAHAWKS' PETE CARROLL

The outcome of a Super Bowl can change in an instant. Head Coach Pete Carroll and the Seattle Seahawks found that out in 2015 when they played the New England Patriots.

Seattle trailed 28–24 with 1:14 to play. That is when Carroll watched Seahawks wide receiver Jermaine Kearse make an amazing catch. He juggled it four times before holding on. Seattle was just five yards from the winning touchdown.

The Seahawks got to the 1-yard line on the next play. That small distance was all that separated them from a second consecutive title. The previous year, they had beaten the Denver Broncos 43–8 to win the Super Bowl.

◄ **Coach Pete Carroll has experienced the best and worst of the Super Bowl with the Seattle Seahawks.**

Seattle had a great rushing attack. Running back Marshawn Lynch was one of the best in the NFL. With less than one yard to go for a championship, most people thought Lynch would get the ball.

"When Jermaine caught that ball, I felt it was meant to be for us," Seattle linebacker Bruce Irvin said. "Oh, no doubt—we're gonna score. Beast Mode. Beast Mode!"[19] Beast Mode was Lynch's nickname.

But Carroll saw that New England's defense was expecting a run. So he decided the Seahawks should throw. Quarterback Russell Wilson dropped back to pass. He tried to throw a short, quick pass to Ricardo Lockette. But Patriots cornerback Malcolm Butler intercepted it. The Patriots ran out the clock to win the Super Bowl.

Viewers around the world were shocked. Carroll took all the blame.

"I made the decision," Carroll said. "I said, 'Throw the ball.' Nobody to blame but me."[20]

Carroll answered the same questions over and over that night. Early the next morning, at 4:50, he awoke. The result of his decision finally hit him fully. He cried. After that, he moved on.

New England Patriots cornerback Malcolm Butler (left) ▶ intercepts the final pass of the Super Bowl on February 1, 2015.

"We did so many beautiful things to get to that point," he later said, "so many positive things that happened, so many players that played so well and coaches that coached so well and on and on and on that that one moment isn't going to define this team and who we are. This is a championship team."[21]

The loss only served to inspire Carroll to once again get his team back to football's biggest stage.

◀ **Carroll took the blame for the play call that led to the game-ending interception.**

GLOSSARY

conference (KON-fer-uhns): A conference is a group of teams. The American Football Conference and National Football Conference have 16 teams each.

drive (dryv): A drive is a team's plays in a possession. The New York Giants had a late touchdown drive to beat the New England Patriots in 2008.

formation (fawr-MEY-shuhn): A formation is the way players line up for a play. The New England Patriots used a strange but legal formation against the Baltimore Ravens in the 2015 playoffs.

Pro Bowl (Pro Bohl): The Pro Bowl is the NFL's all star game, in which the season's best players compete. New York Giants receiver David Tyree made the Pro Bowl as a special teams player in 2005.

replay (REE-pley): A replay is video footage sometimes used by referees to confirm calls. Bill Vinovich worked as a replay official before getting back on the field as a referee.

sacking (SAK-ing): Sacking a quarterback is tackling him behind the line of scrimmage. The New England Patriots were close to sacking Eli Manning before he threw his famous pass to David Tyree in 2008.

safety (SAYF-tee): A safety is a defensive player in football primarily responsible for guarding receivers downfield. Safety Rodney Harrison tried to stop David Tyree from making his famous catch in 2008.

streak (streek): A streak is something that happens over and over without interruption. Some members of The Never Miss a Super Bowl Club have kept their streak of going to games intact since 1967.

SOURCE NOTES

1-2. Sherry Phillips. "Q&A with Never Miss a Super Bowl Club." *American Profile*. PGOA Media. 3 Feb. 2011. Web. 5 May 2015.

3-4. David Greene. "Dedicated Fans Have Never Missed a Super Bowl." *NPR*. NPR. 4 Feb. 2012. Web. 5 May 2015.

5. Jodi Weigand. "Pennsylvania Man Heads to His 49th Super Bowl." *The Morning Call*. Tribune Publishing. 31 Jan. 2015. Web. 5 May 2015.

6. Tim Layden. "Remember?" *Sports Illustrated*. Time Inc. 4 Aug. 2008. Web. 7 May 2015.

7. Tim Layden. "They're History." *Sports Illustrated*. Time Inc. 11 Feb. 2008. Web. 7 May 2015.

8-9. Tim Layden. 4 Aug. 2008.

10. Peter King. "'Joy Wells up in My Heart.'" *Sports Illustrated*. Time Inc. 29 Jan. 2015. Web. 7 May 2015.

11. Austin Murphy. "Bland Bands, Nip Slips and 3-D Bebop." *Sports Illustrated*. Time Inc. 3 Feb. 2014. Web. 7 May 2015.

12-13. Les Carpenter. "How U2's Masterful New Orleans Performances for NFL Almost Never Happened." *Yahoo!*. Yahoo. 30 Jan. 2013. Web. 7 May 2015.

14-16. Peter King. "A Super Bowl Comeback." *Sports Illustrated*. Time Inc. 26 Jan. 2015. Web. 7 May 2015.

17. "NRL: Ref Inspected Footballs Properly in AFC Title Game." *The New York Times*. The New York Times Company. 29 Jan. 2015. Web. 7 May 2015.

18. Peter King. 26 Jan. 2015.

19. Michael Silver. "Seahawks' Pete Carroll Explains Ill-Fated Call in Super Bowl XLIX." *NFL*. NFL Enterprises. 2 Feb. 2015. Web. 7 May 2015.

20. Eddie Pells. "Carroll: 'Nobody to Blame but Me.'" *The Salt Lake Tribune*. MediaNews Group. 1 Feb. 2015. Web. 5 May 2015.

21. Chuck Schilken. "Pete Carroll Says He Cried in Bed Following Super Bowl Loss." *Los Angeles Times*. Tribune Publishing. 21 Jun. 2015. Web. 7 May 2015.

TO LEARN MORE

Books

Anastasio, Dina. *What Is the Super Bowl?* New York: Grosset & Dunlap, 2015.

Bryant, Howard. *Legends: The Best Players, Games, and Teams in Football.* New York: Philomel Books, 2015.

Christopher, Matt. *The Super Bowl.* New York: Little, Brown, and Co., 2006.

Web Sites

Visit our Web site for links about the Super Bowl: childsworld.com/links

Note to Parents, Teachers, and Librarians: We routinely verify our Web links to make sure they are safe and active sites. So encourage your readers to check them out!

INDEX